SOLVING YOUR INNER CONFLICT

THE WORKBOOK

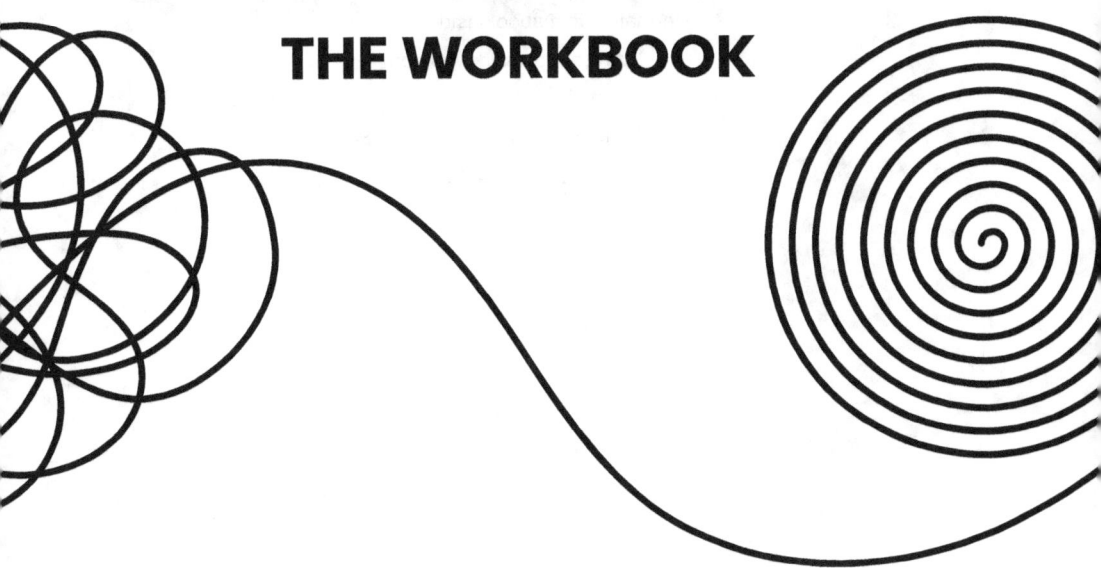

By
Judd Batchelor

Copyright © 2022
Judd Batchelor

All rights reserved. No part of this publication may be produced, distributed, or transmitted in any form or by any means, including photocopying, recording, or other electronic or mechanical methods, without the prior written permision of the publisher, except in the case of brief quotations embodied in critical reviews and certain other noncommercial uses permitted by copyright law.

For permission requests, write to the publisher, addressed "Attention: Permissions Coordinator" at the email address below:

Life and Success Media Ltd

e-mail: info@abookinsideyou.com

www.abookinsideyou.com

ISBN Number: 978-1-7398859-3-9

Cover Design: **MIA**Design.com

CONTENTS

FROM THE AUTHOR	4
INTRO	5
HOW TO USE THIS BOOK	6
THE OUTCOME	7
RESPECTING OUR DIFFERENCES	
DEALING WITH PREJUDICE	17
HOW TO BE A SUPPORTIVE FRIEND	27
DEALING WITH FRUSTRATIONS, BOREDOM, ISOLATION	35
DEBATES, ARGUMENTS	39
SEARCHING FOR THE WORD	51
BODY LANGUAGE	55
7 DAYS OF THOUGHT DIARY	59
FEELING SAFE IN YOUR SURROUNDINGS	67
GOOD RELATIONSHIPS	69
VISION BOARD	71
SOLVING YOUR INNER CONFLICT	79

From the Author

Hi there,

I hope you enjoyed watching A Mother Speaks online.

This workbook was created to encourage you to see that there are always two sides to every person, situation and decision. When I wrote 'A Mother speaks' in 2006/07, I was a struggling actor who just wanted to show the world how talented I was. So I needed something that would showcase my range - something that showed how well I could portray; joy, pain, anger, frustration, and love. And like magic, I would win an Oscar or BAFTA. Nope, that didn't happen! But that was one side of the coin, and here's the other. When I performed the play, the story resonated with everyone. The laughter and deep sighs from the audience when they saw themselves in the character, or sadly the tears from the parents and family members whose true story I was telling. I realized that this story was not for my own vanity and ego but for the lives it will help to change, and that's when I began to see its message another way.

Intro

A Mother Speaks, the workbook is for you to look at your own inner conflicts and create a pathway to solve them or at least see them in another way.

The popular meaning of Conflict Resolution states: **Conflict resolution is the process in which two or more parties work toward a solution to a problem or dispute. The parties involved work to achieve a solution that solves the problem in a productive way.**

In the case of this workbook and how it relates to the story of A Mother Speaks, the mother made that fatal choice in a moment of uncalculated madness to take matters into her own hands. As a result, she is now forever trying to deal with her inner conflicts. So before you can resolve your relationships with others, look within first. (That's what I'm doing daily!)

How to use this Book

This workbook is designed for you to refer to over time, it's not meant to be finished in one gulp (like a whole bottle of water, when you've just finished a workout!) Please take your time.

The blank pages and spaces in this workbook are for you to fulfil. When an actor is given a script you would get a neatly presented typed up document, and by the time that actor is ready to go on stage or in front of a camera, that script is usually COVERED in notes. These notes are vital to the actor because it informs them of what is really going on inside the mind of the character.

- Why did she say that?
- Why did he leave the room?
- What is my motive?

1

THE OUTCOME

What do you want the outcome to be in these scenarios?

Dreaming about a Lion

A Lion is approaching you; he looks friendly, but as everyone knows, Lions are the kings of the jungle and anything moving in their jungle is their dinner.

You have a superpower that you could use to defeat the lion or tame it. Choose your superpower and the outcome of this dream:

Suggested Super powers:

1. You can become invisible
2. You can change into another animal
3. You can jump really high
4. You can talk to animals
5. You are fearless
6. You can turn yourself into; Fire,air,water
7. You can become blind

Solving Your Inner Conflicts

8. You can run fast
9. You can fly
10. You can see through any solid object

You don't have to use these suggestions; you may have one of your own. But chose wisely because you want to get out alive.

I was walking through the jungle on a bright summers day...

THE OUTCOME

Solving Your Inner Conflicts

The Outcome 2

I have had many situations in my life that I look back on and wish for a better outcome. So many times when I said to myself, "Why didn't I say something?" "Why did I listen to him?" "I should've minded my own business."

Has there been a time that you could've chosen a better outcome? Has your chosen outcome changed your life for better or worse?

Write about that situation and give it a different version. Remember to protect the names of any individuals involved!

Start:

_____
_____
_____
_____
_____
_____
_____
_____
_____

Solving Your Inner Conflicts

The Outcome 3

The Actor Vs The Comedian
Please Google – The Oscars Will & Chris

This scenario made the headlines in 2022. It was all over the news and social media. The setting for this scenario was on the world's biggest, glitziest, glamorous night ever.

The players in this scenario are known worldwide. We've enjoyed watching them as superheroes. They have made us laugh and cry.

Who am I talking about? I'm afraid I cannot reveal the names, but let's just call them Person A, B, and C. I will give you four versions to choose the best outcome.

A, B & C are all at this glittery night of awards and celebrations. Person A is the host for the night. Person A is also a comedian. Most comedians make jokes about anyone or anything. They can turn the most negative thing into humour.

B&C, who are married, are in the audience. Person B is up for an award and is so far enjoying the night. Person A is busy cracking jokes and the audience is loving it. Person C has been going through some life changes and is vulnerable about how they look. Remember, AB&C are very famous, and so are their lives. So basically, everyone knows their

Solving Your Inner Conflicts

story. Person A decides to make a joke about Person C's appearance, and this angers Person B; this angers him so much that he goes onto the stage in front of millions of viewers and SLAPS Person A.

A, B & C are all at this glittery night of awards and celebrations. Person A is the host for the night. Person A is also a comedian. Most comedians make jokes about anyone or anything, they can turn the most negative thing into humour.

B&C, who are married, are in the audience, Person B is up for an award and is so far enjoying the night. Person A is busy cracking jokes, and the audience is loving it. Person C has been going through some life changes and is vulnerable about how they look. Remember, AB&C are very famous, and so are their lives. So basically everyone knows their story. Person A decides to make a joke about Person C's appearance, and this angers Person B, but he decides to calm down at that moment and wait until the show is over; then, he goes backstage and SLAPS person A.

A, B & C are all at this glittery night of awards and celebrations. Person A is the host for the night, Person A is also a comedian. Most comedian make jokes about anyone or anything, they can turn the most negative thing into humour.

B&C who are married are in the audience, Person B is up for an award and is so far enjoying the night. Person A is busy cracking jokes and the audience is loving it. Person C has been going through some life changes and is vanurable about the way they look. Remember AB&C are very famous and so

THE OUTCOME

is their lives, so basically everyone knows their story. Person A decides to make a joke about Person C's appearance, and this angers Person B, so he decides to heckle him back and make a joke about Person A's appearance. He does this so well that the whole audience begins to laugh at person A.

A, B & C are all at this glittery night of awards and celebrations. Person A is the host for the night, Person A is also a comedian. Most comedians make jokes about anyone or anything; they can turn the most negative thing into humour.

B&C, who are married, are in the audience, Person B is up for an award and is so far enjoying the night. Person A is busy cracking jokes, and the audience is loving it. Person C has been going through some life changes and is vulnerable about the way they look. Remember, AB&C are very famous, and so are their lives. So basically, everyone knows their story. Person A makes a joke about Person C's appearance, which angers Person B, but he decides to calm down and wait until the end of the glitzy awards ceremony and talk to him backstage. His aim is to seek an apology.

Solving Your Inner Conflicts

2

RESPECTING OUR DIFFERENCES DEALING WITH PREJUDICE

Ok, look at this heading, and ask yourself, "Do I honestly respect other peoples differences?" "Am I prejudice?"

Circle **Yes** or **No** to these questions

Would you sit next to a person that perhaps looked unkempt?

Yes or **No** Write your reason.

_____

_____

_____

_____

Solving Your Inner Conflicts

_____
_____
_____
_____
_____
_____

Would you smile at a stranger or wish them a pleasant day?

Yes or **No** Write your reason.

_____
_____
_____
_____
_____
_____
_____
_____

RESPECTING OUR DIFFERENCES/DEALING WITH PREJUDICE

Would you help someone who struggled with pronouncing a word because English is their second language?

Yes or **No** Write your reason

_____
_____
_____
_____
_____
_____
_____
_____

Does someone wearing nice clothes seem trustworthy?

Yes or **No** Write your reason.

_____
_____
_____
_____
_____

Solving Your Inner Conflicts

_____
_____
_____
_____
_____
_____

Have you tried different food from different cultures?

Yes or **No**   List the countries

_____
_____
_____
_____
_____
_____
_____
_____
_____
_____

RESPECTING OUR DIFFERENCES/DEALING WITH PREJUDICE

Have you ever disagreed with a best friend/family in the past?

Yes or **No**   Explain what happen

_____

_____

_____

_____

_____

_____

_____

_____

_____

_____

_____

_____

_____

_____

Solving Your Inner Conflicts

Do you still disagree with your best friend/family?

Yes or **No**

If you answered Yes, explain why? If you answered No, what changed your mind?

_____
_____
_____
_____
_____
_____
_____
_____
_____
_____
_____
_____
_____
_____
_____
_____

RESPECTING OUR DIFFERENCES/DEALING WITH PREJUDICE

A young boy of 19yrs old was found stabbed on March 17th… (she stops reading aloud and reads the article to herself, then she looks back at the audience) What's the point in me reading you the rest… you already know the story… you see it on the news nearly every week, I mean walking past a bunch of flowers stuck on a railing, has become as common as walking past a tramp begging! A Mother Speaks ©

If you saw this bunch of flowers stuck on a railing what do you automatically think? Tick the answer and explain your choice

○ Murder

○ Accident

Explain why

Solving Your Inner Conflicts

RESPECTING OUR DIFFERENCES/DEALING WITH PREJUDICE

If you saw a bunch of flowers stuck on a railing, would you automatically think it was a male person that died?

Yes or **No**

Explain why

Solving Your Inner Conflicts

3

HOW TO BE A SUPPORTIVE FRIEND

Solving Your Inner Conflicts

A supportive friend understands who you are and what you need. You will quickly learn they will be with you through thick and thin. You both will go through some tough times and some very good times. However, a simple thing such as a fight isn't going to hold you two back from a healthy friendship.

Have you ever had the phone ring and it's your friend calling? They start the conversation by explaining what has happened to them; they don't even take a breath! And they don't even ask you how you're doing?? It just seems to be all about them. The other side is that you're also having a bad day. How do you tell your friend that you're not in the mood to listen? Or do you say nothing and just listen?

What do you say?

_____

_____

_____

_____

_____

_____

_____

_____

HOW TO BE A SUPPORTIVE FRIEND

When you need support what are your thoughts?

"My friends should know me well enough to tell that I'm bothered about something."

"I wish people would leave me alone,
I'll figure this out myself."

"I need a hug."

"No one cares about me anyway."

"I want all my friends to stop what
they're doing and pay attention to me."

"I'm afraid to show my weakness to people."

"I'm always supporting others."

"Maybe my friends have problems of their own."

Postive traits & Negative traits

Think of four important people in your life and list all the things you like about them and all the things you don't.

Solving Your Inner Conflicts

Friend 1

_____
_____
_____
_____
_____
_____
_____

Friend 2

_____
_____
_____
_____
_____
_____
_____

Friend 3

Friend 4

Solving Your Inner Conflicts

Everyone said it was a huge turnout at the funeral. All his friends from college and his old school... everyone. But I couldn't see them or even think about the crowds of friends and family... all I could think about was you.... Surprised? Just imagine it was my son's last day on this earth,
 but all I could see was you.

A Mother Speaks ©

How would you support someone in these scenarios

_____
_____
_____
_____
_____
_____
_____

Your friend is in a heated argument, they are in the wrong, how do you support them?

_____
_____
_____
_____

HOW TO BE A SUPPORTIVE FRIEND

Your friend is gravely ill, they only have a few months to live. How do you support them?

Solving Your Inner Conflicts

Your friend is being bullied at work or school, how do you support them?

_____
_____
_____
_____
_____
_____
_____

How do you support a friend that's been lying?

_____
_____
_____
_____
_____
_____
_____

4

DEALING WITH FRUSTRATIONS, BOREDOM, ISOLATION

Most conflicts with others stem from some form of frustration with yourself, your situation in life, and what you want from the person you're in conflict with. Are you the type of person that says, "People just don't understand me?"

Some common reasons for boredom are lack of motivation, not knowing what you want from life, a high opinion of yourself, so everything is beneath you, and laziness. Are you the type of person that causes disruption and arguments because you're bored? And do you think a good/heated debate is exciting?

Isolation, feeling left out? I really want things my way, so I won't take part. I have nothing in common with these

Solving Your Inner Conflicts

people. I want to speak up, but I'm scared of what people may think. Do you often feel left out? Have you ever isolated someone from your group?

Can you relate to any of the above?

Write about a time when you experienced these feelings of Frustration, Boredom, and Isolation, On the other side, make up a solution.

_____

_____

_____

_____

_____

_____

_____

_____

_____

_____

_____

_____

_____

DEALING WITH FRUSTRATIONS, BOREDOM, ISOLATION

Solving Your Inner Conflicts

5

DEBATES, ARGUMENTS

Think of times when you were having a debate, which turned into an argument. Or has it just been a full-blown argument? Now I'm not suggesting that you must have had arguments. You could be a very agreeable happy person. So if this is you, then skip this part. But if you are being truthful, then go ahead.

Write about the times (that you can remember) you got into an argument, and write the scenario from start to finish. After you have finished writing and thinking about the argument, tick under the heading that most applies. Once you've done this, come back and review your answers. Is there a pattern? Or are you able to see both sides?

Solving Your Inner Conflicts

Argument/debate	Not worth the argument, I was wrong	This argument was fully justified, I was right
Argument 1		
Argument 2		
Argument 3		
Argument 4		
Argument 5		
Argument 6		
Argument 7		
Argument 8		
Argument 9		
Argument 10		

Argument 1

Argument 2

Argument 3

Argument 4

Argument 5

Argument 6

Argument 7

Argument 8

Argument 9

Argument 10

6

SEARCHING FOR THE WORD

Solving Your Inner Conflicts

Keywords for a Good Outcome

R	E	S	P	E	C	T	X	C	M
E	Y	T	I	R	G	E	T	N	I
S	C	A	G	W	X	B	Y	I	V
O	O	S	S	E	N	M	L	A	C
L	L	P	O	T	F	Q	I	Z	P
U	L	V	H	K	L	W	S	U	A
T	A	H	O	N	E	S	T	Y	T
I	B	P	J	H	O	Z	E	L	I
O	O	Y	U	G	T	Y	N	A	E
N	R	C	D	F	S	X	I	E	N
D	A	J	S	E	U	O	V	U	C
J	T	Z	T	D	R	I	F	H	E
K	E	X	E	C	T	W	K	T	Q
R	G	H	P	R	X	P	R	D	Z
M	E	F	E	M	P	A	T	H	Y
Y	A	S	L	B	Y	V	P	M	V
D	S	Q	I	A	Z	O	N	P	C
A	P	R	Z	C	E	E	R	G	A

Agree   Resolution   Honesty
Patience   Collaborate   Respect
Assertive   Calmness   Trust
Integrity   Listen   Empathy

SEARCHING FOR THE WORD

Keywords For A Negative Outcome

J	K	C	W	U	C	I	D	K	A
A	W	O	B	N	O	T	I	I	R
N	C	L	B	S	N	V	S	P	G
T	O	D	C	Y	F	E	A	P	U
I	P	B	H	M	L	E	G	W	M
S	L	A	O	P	I	H	R	Z	E
O	E	T	S	A	C	M	E	E	N
C	V	C	T	T	T	N	E	V	T
I	I	K	I	H	I	O	G	O	A
A	T	D	L	E	N	X	C	R	T
L	A	D	E	T	G	X	F	P	I
X	B	R	K	I	K	T	F	P	V
B	M	M	M	C	O	N	U	A	E
H	O	X	J	V	I	A	N	S	L
T	C	Q	U	D	M	T	W	I	O
R	Y	C	Q	U	Z	S	A	D	V
X	T	L	U	J	C	I	H	G	R
O	P	P	O	S	E	D	E	H	Y

Disapprove   Counter   Hostile
Conflicting   Argumentative   Unfavorable
Opposed   Distant   Combative
Antisocial   Cold   Resisting
Unsympathetic Disagree

Solving Your Inner Conflicts

7

BODY LANGUAGE

Are you like me? Sometimes when I observe people talking from a distance, I often wonder what they're saying. I don't know if its' the creative in me always thinking, "I could write a film about this!" Have you ever seen a heated argument between two people? The way the skin tone can change colour with rage, or the eyes become wide and fixed on the other person, and the arms and hands are either fixed tightly folded or waving about!

If you're at a distance and can't really hear what's been said, you can't tell who started the argument, who's in the wrong or right, who's lying, and who's the leader.

Look at these two images and write out the scenario:

Solving Your Inner Conflicts

What happened?

_____
_____
_____
_____
_____
_____
_____
_____
_____
_____

BODY LANGUAGE

What happened?

Solving Your Inner Conflicts

8

7 DAYS OF THOUGHT DIARY

Write a word or sentence within the thought bubble, or find the image and stick it in the thought bubble. The days don't have to run one after the other. It's just 7 days of thought.

Remember, people say things like

"Your thoughts become things."

"What you think about, you bring about."

"Mind over matter."

"Be careful what you wish for."

"What were you thinking!"

"next time, think before you speak."

Day 1
Write the time

Day 2

Solving Your Inner Conflicts

Day 3

Day 4

Solving Your Inner Conflicts

Day 5

Day 6

Solving Your Inner Conflicts

Day 7

5

FEELING SAFE IN YOUR SURROUNDINGS

I had a dream once where I was dressed in a white body suit and was walking across this narrow ledge attached to a huge billboard up high off the ground. I didn't want to walk across, but this woman insisted I walk across to meet her. All I felt was fear! I didn't want to slip and fall. I really hated this dream and was glad when I woke up.

Sadly some bad situations are not dreams; they are someone's reality. For example, a person's first day at work or school can feel like the dream I had.

List some things that make you feel fearful and unsafe. How could you overcome that problem?

Solving Your Inner Conflicts

My fear is…

___

I will solve it by…

___

6

GOOD RELATIONSHIPS

In your opinion, what makes a good relationship?

_____
_____
_____
_____
_____
_____
_____
_____
_____
_____
_____
_____

Solving Your Inner Conflicts

7

VISION BOARD

Things you will need.

- Newspapers
- Magazines
- The internet
- Scissors
- Glue/ cello tape

These few blank pages are for you to collect positive affirmations, quotes, and pictures of things that will uplift and inspire you. Stick them onto the blank pages or write in interesting quote or words that you like.

Solving Your Inner Conflicts

VISION BOARD

Solving Your Inner Conflicts

VISION BOARD

Solving Your Inner Conflicts

VISION BOARD

Solving Your Inner Conflicts

8
SOLVING YOUR INNER CONFLICT

Well, we have come to the end of this workbook. But we are really at the beginning because now you can put what you've learned about yourself into practice.

And by the way, what have you learned about yourself? Any revelations that you didn't see coming?

List some of the changes you plan to make.

_____

_____

_____

_____

_____

_____

Solving Your Inner Conflicts

www.ingramcontent.com/pod-product-compliance
Lightning Source LLC
Chambersburg PA
CBHW072105110526
44590CB00018B/3326